Living

Homemade Marshmallows

Marshmallows were originally made from the root of the marshmallow plant; today, corn syrup and sugar are the main ingredients. Homemade ones can be cut into any shape you like.

INGREDIENTS

Makes about 40.

- 2 1/2 tablespoons unflavored gelatin
- 1 1/2 cups granulated sugar
- 1 cup light corn syrup
- 1/4 teaspoon salt
- 2 tablespoons pure vanilla extract
- Confectioners' sugar, for dusting

DIRECTIONS

1. Combine gelatin and 1/2 cup cold water in the bowl of an electric mixer with whisk attachment. Let stand 30 minutes.

2. Combine granulated sugar, corn syrup, salt, and 1/2 cup water in a small heavy saucepan; place over low heat, and stir until sugar has dissolved. Wash down sides of pan with a wet pastry brush to dissolve sugar crystals.

3. Clip on a candy thermometer; raise heat to high. Cook syrup without stirring until it reaches 244 degrees.(firm-ball stage). Immediately remove pan from heat.

4. With mixer on low speed, slowly and carefully pour syrup into the softened gelatin. Increase speed to high; beat until mixture is very thick and white and has almost tripled in volume, about 15 minutes. Add vanilla; beat to incorporate.

5. Generously dust an 8-by-12-inch glass baking pan with confectioners' sugar. Pour marshmallow mixture into pan. Dust top with confectioners' sugar; wet your hands, and pat it to smooth. Dust with confectioners' sugar; let stand overnight, uncovered, to dry out. Turn out onto a board; cut marshmallows with a dry hot knife into 1 1/2-inch squares, and dust with more confectioners' sugar.

First published

A1Books.com
35 Love Lane
Netcong NJ   07857

Ordered By: KELLY DENEEN
BOSTON COLLEGE LAW LIBRARY
885 CENTRE STREET
NEWTON CENTRE, MA
02459

Received By: KELLY DENEEN
BOSTON COLLEGE LAW LIBRARY
885 CENTRE STREET
NEWTON CENTRE, MA
02459

Shipping Date	Shipped Via	P.O. #	Order #
08/19/08	Economy Mail		ABE16583308

Product ID	Description	Shipped Qty	Unit Price	Extended Price
9780486417981	2600 TYPOGRAPHIC ORNAMENTS & D	1		
Customer Service	http://support.a1books.com			

Thank you for shopping at A1Books.com. Customer Service -
http://support.a1books.com

Telephone: Email:

RETURN LABEL

FROM:

KELLY DENEEN
BOSTON COLLEGE LAW LIBRARY
885 CENTRE STREET
NEWTON CENTRE, MA
02459

Please use the supplied return labels on the outside of your returned package.

TO: ABE16583308

A1BOOKS.COM-CDF
35 LOVE LN
NETCONG
      NJ   07857-1013

D024 - 05133V00

NV   089 #699F0   20C8081   08/19/08 47324154

2600 Typographic Ornaments & Designs

selected and arranged by

Maggie Kate

DOVER PUBLICATIONS, INC.
Mineola, New York

Bibliographical Note

2600 Typographic Ornaments and Designs, first published in 2001, is a compilation of most of the material from *Allerlei Zierat: Zur Ausstattung Von Drucksachen Jeden Charakters,* originally published in Leipzig, c. 1902, by J. G. Schelter & Giesecke. The contents have been selected and arranged by Maggie Kate. And an introductory Note has been specially prepared for this edition.

DOVER *Pictorial Archive* SERIES

Library of Congress Cataloging-in-Publication Data

Kate, Maggie.
    2600 typographic ornaments and designs / selected and arranged by Maggie Kate.
        p. cm. — (Dover pictorial archive series)
    "A compilation of most of the material from Allerlei Zierat: zur Ausstattung von Drucksachen jeden Charakters, originally published in Leipzig, c. 1902 by J. G. Schelter & Giesecke."
    ISBN 0-486-41798-0
    1. Type ornaments—Specimens. 2. Printers' ornaments—Specimens. 3. J. G. Schelter & Giesecke. 4. Type and type-founding—Germany—Liepzig—History. I. Title: Two thousand six hundred typographic ornaments and designs. II. J. G. Schelter & Giesecke. Allerlei Zierat: zur Ausstattung von Drucksachen jeden Charakters. III. Title. IV. Series.

Z250.3 .K38 2001
686.2'24—dc21

                      2001032351

Manufactured in the United States of America
Dover Publications, Inc., 31 East 2nd Street, Mineola, N.Y. 11501

NOTE

This richly diverse compendium of typographical ornaments is culled from a turn-of-the-century catalog of the German foundry established in 1819 in Leipzig by punchcutter Johann Schelter and typefounder Christian Giesecke. Catalogs such as theirs were made possible by the invention of electrotype around 1850, and they offered for sale to printing jobbers a tremendous assortment of printer's ornaments, as well as cast type in various faces. The cost of each ornament varied from fifteen cents to three dollars, depending on size. Ever since the invention of the printing press in the fifteenth century, printers have used decorative ornaments to fill space in page layouts and enliven the printed page. These designs can be distinguished from illustrations in that they have no connection with the content of the text, being purely decorative.

Many of the items contained herein show the influence of the Art Nouveau movement in the applied and decorative arts that flourished on the continent around the same time this catalog was published. In Germany, "Art Nouveau" (new art) was known as "Jugendstil"—or youth style—after the magazine *Jugend* (youth). The style was characterized by dominant undulating lines or contours to which all other elements (like color, form, and texture) were secondary, and it was greeted as a new and revitalizing force in the arts. The origins of the movement are manifold, encompassing a broad spectrum of influences including William Morris' Arts and Crafts movement of the 1870s, which sought to grant crafts the same status as that accorded to painting and sculpture. In turn, this movement—which so highly valued the expression of individuality inherent in handicrafts—was at least in part a reaction against the new machine age of mass production heralded by the Industrial Revolution.

This volume has been assembled with the idea in mind of maximum usability for contemporary artists and craftspeople. The ornaments and designs make an attractive complement to typography in all types of printed material, including books, letterheads, newsletters, and package design. They also may be used anywhere that small and elegant designs are required—in needlework and leathercraft, for example.

2

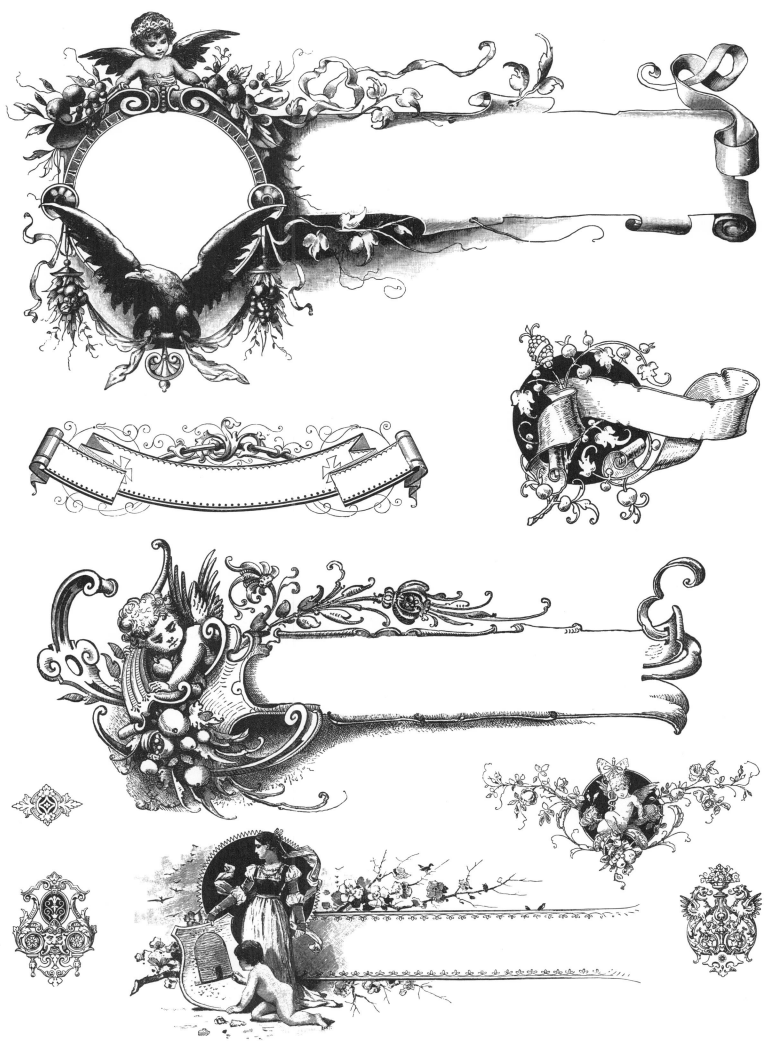

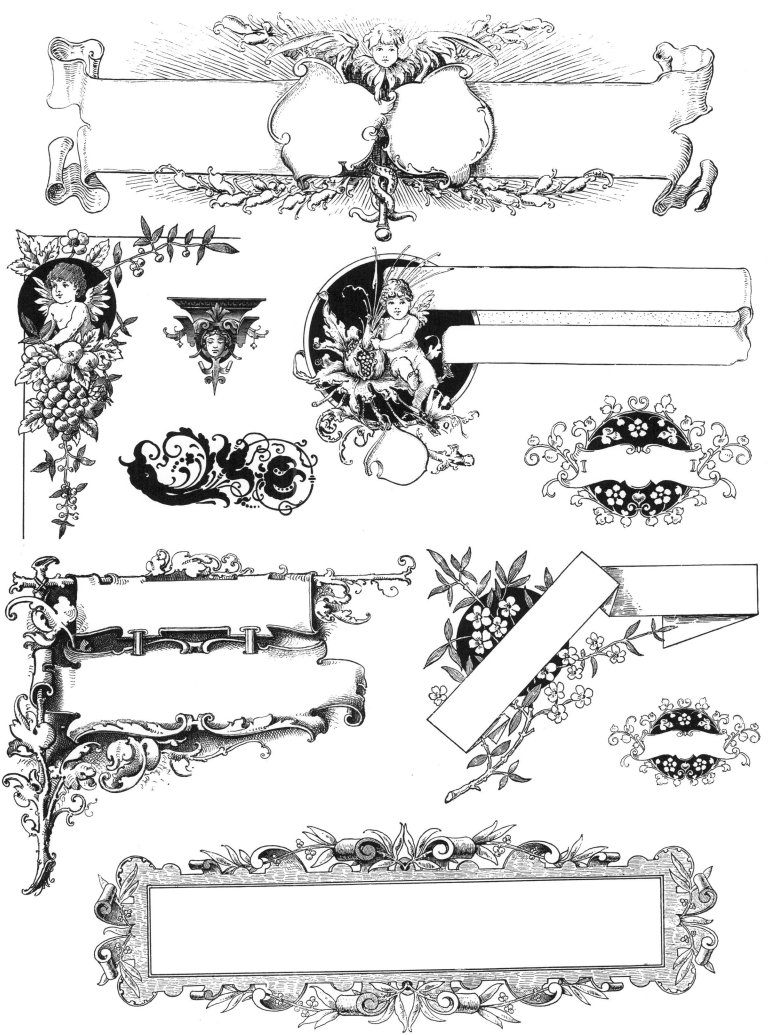

6

9

12

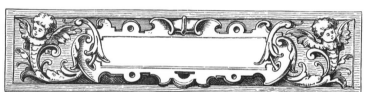

20

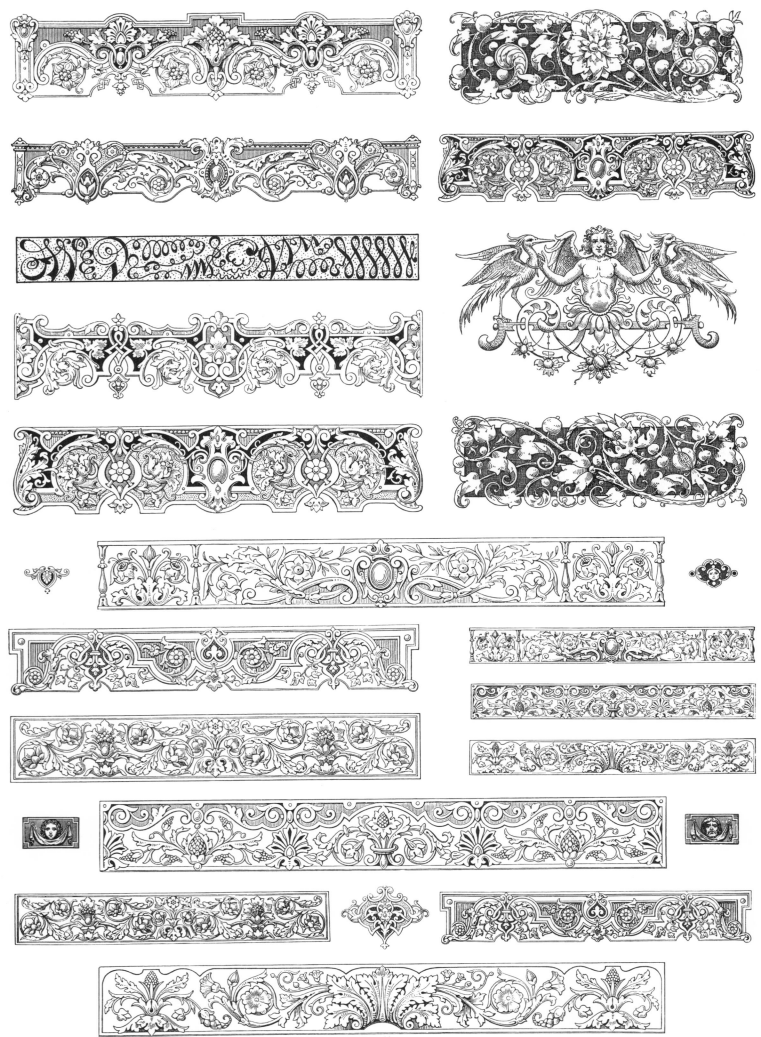

22

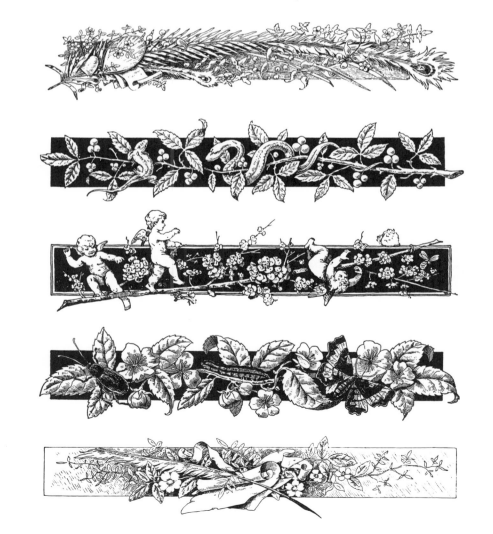

23

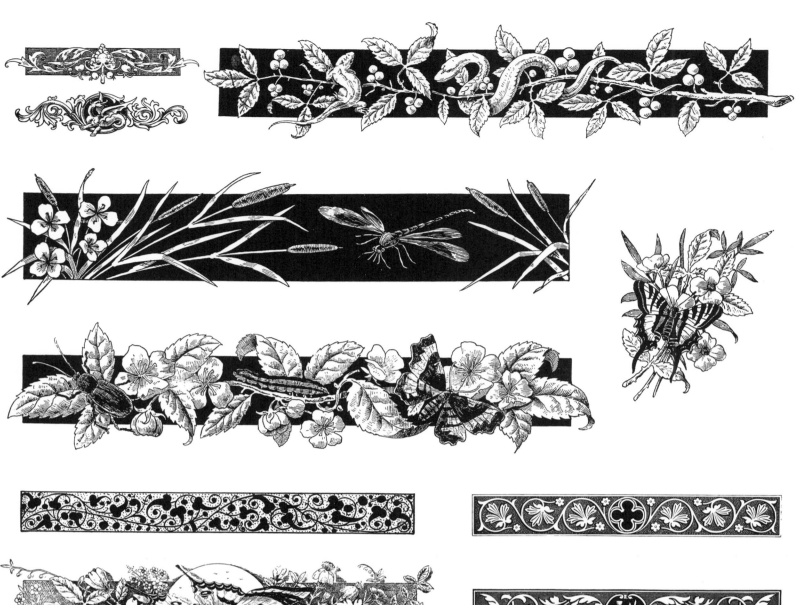

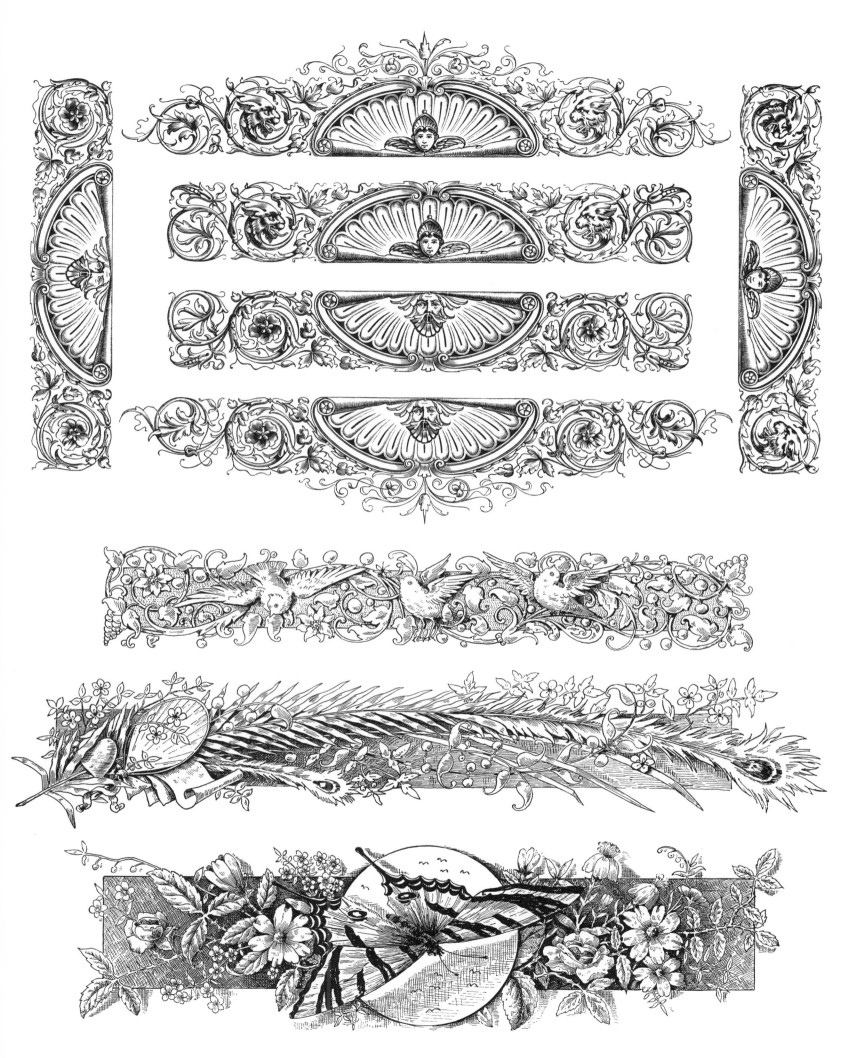

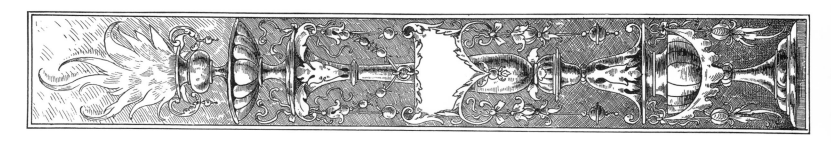

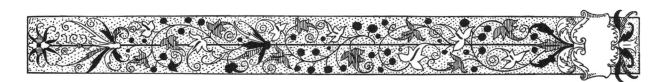

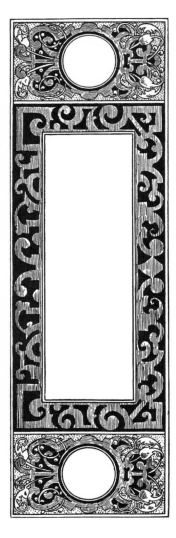

34

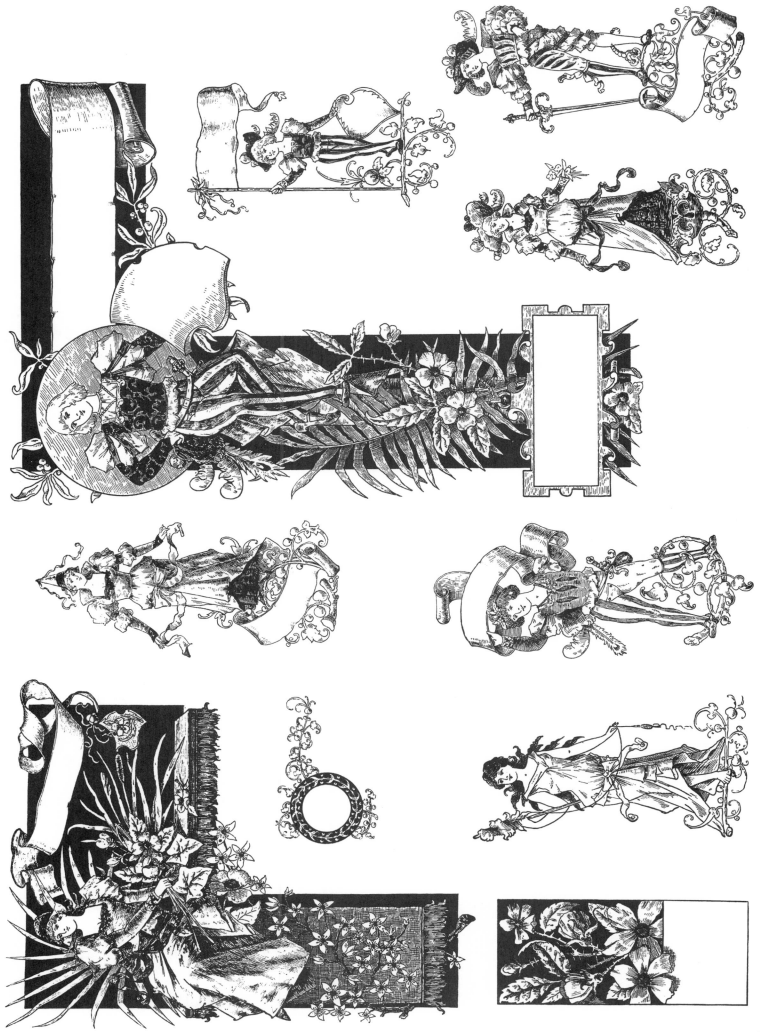

38

39

42

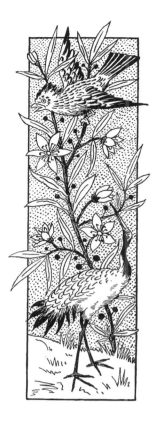

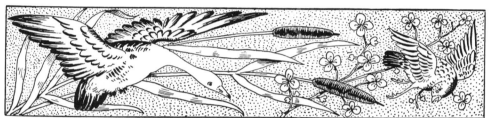
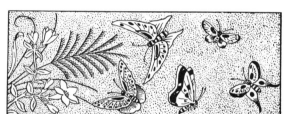

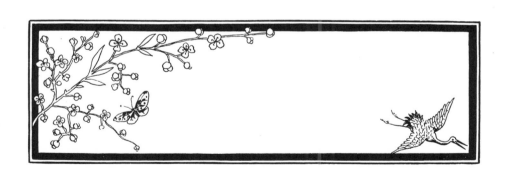

45

51

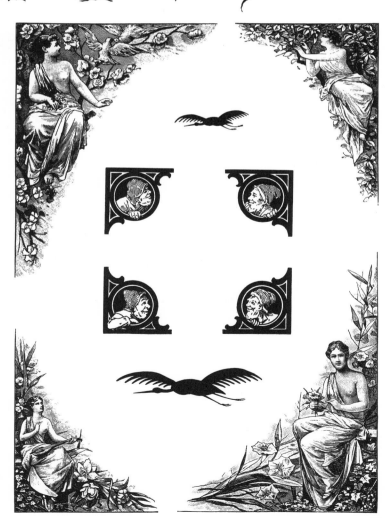

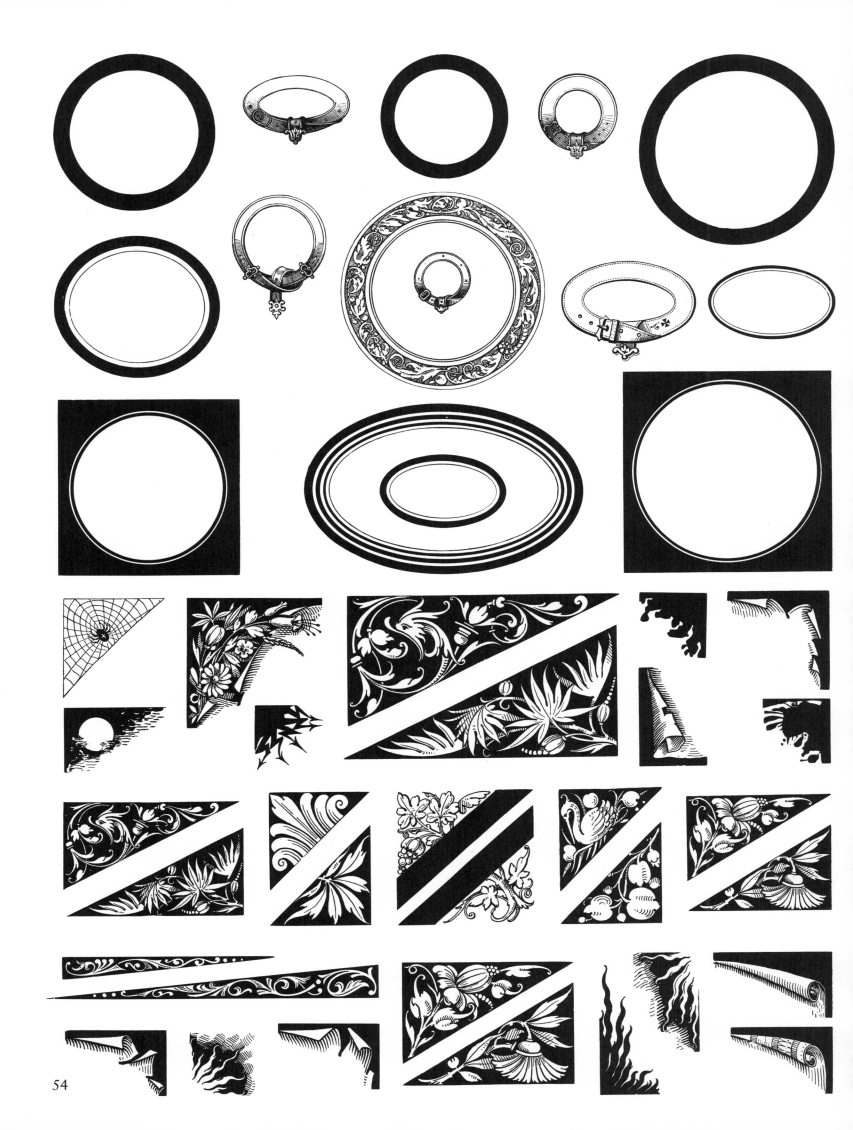

56

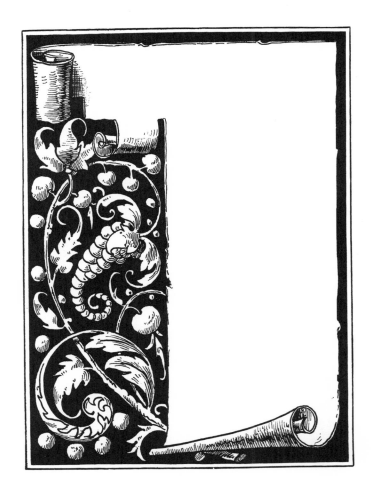

MENU

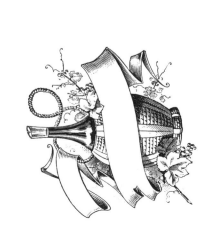

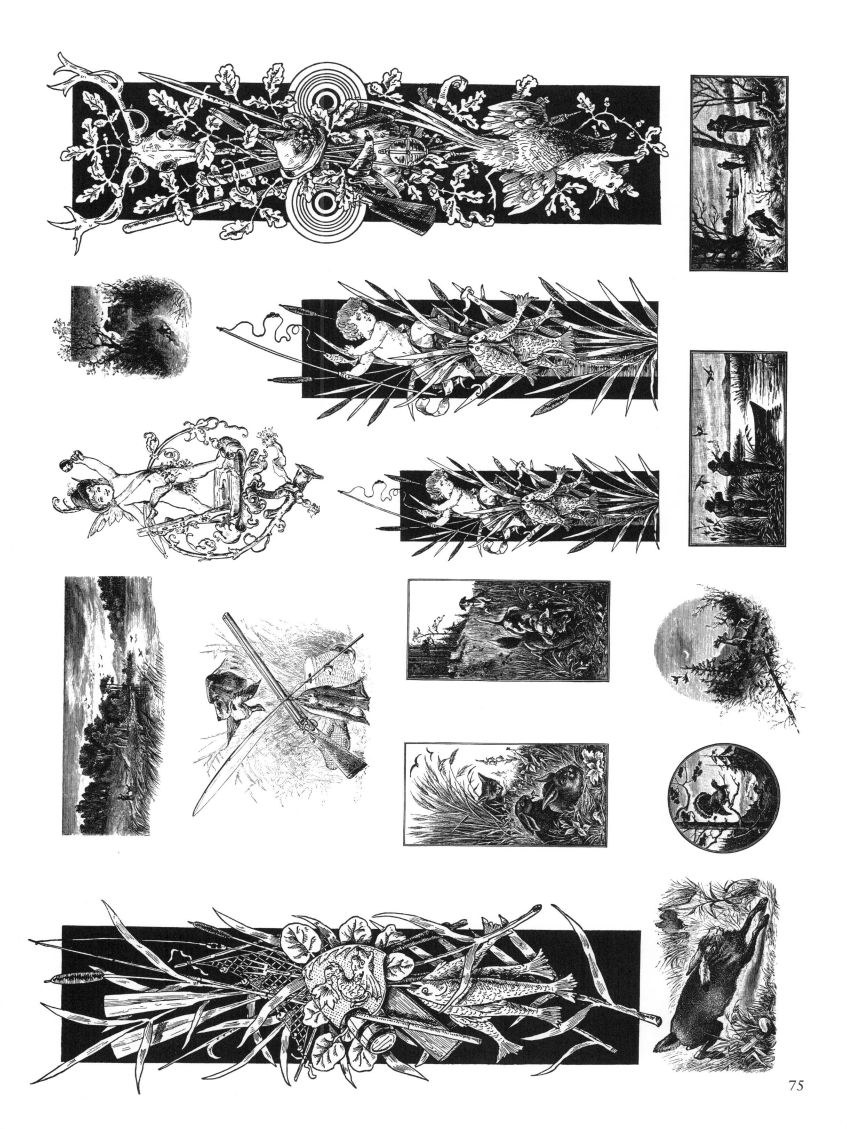

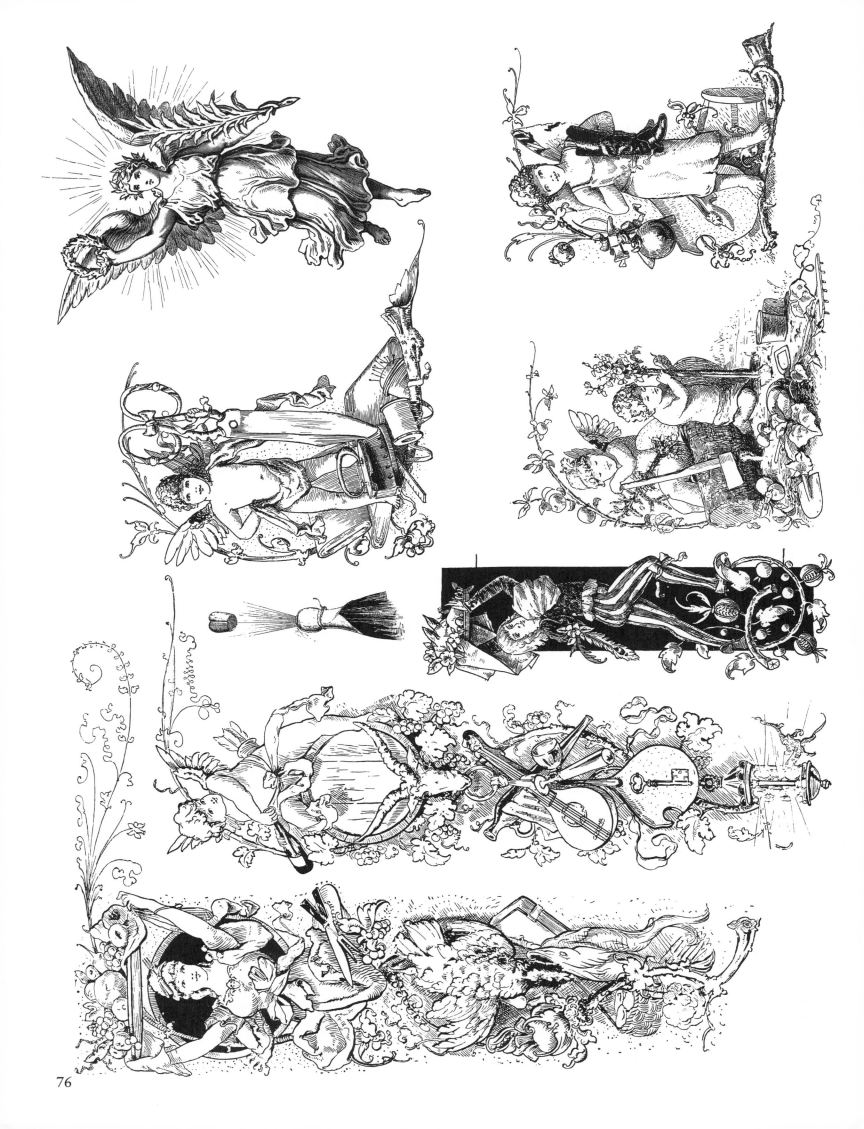

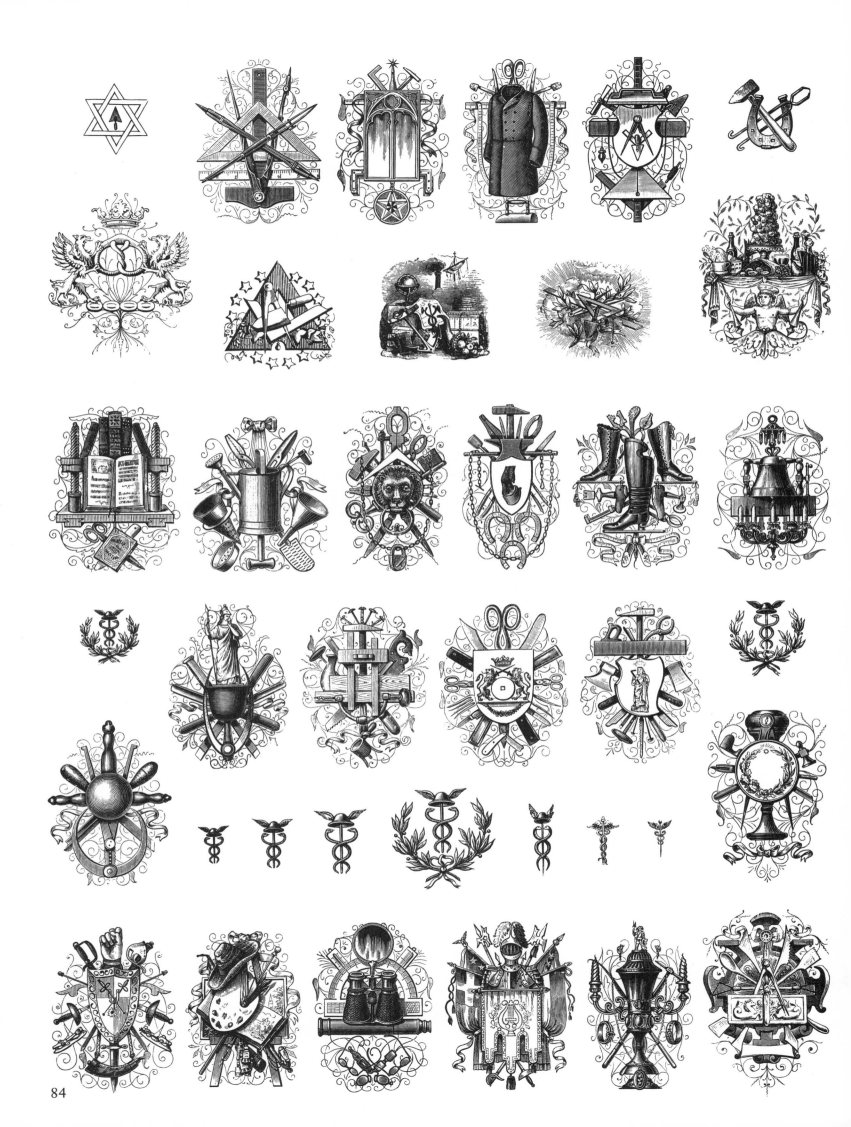

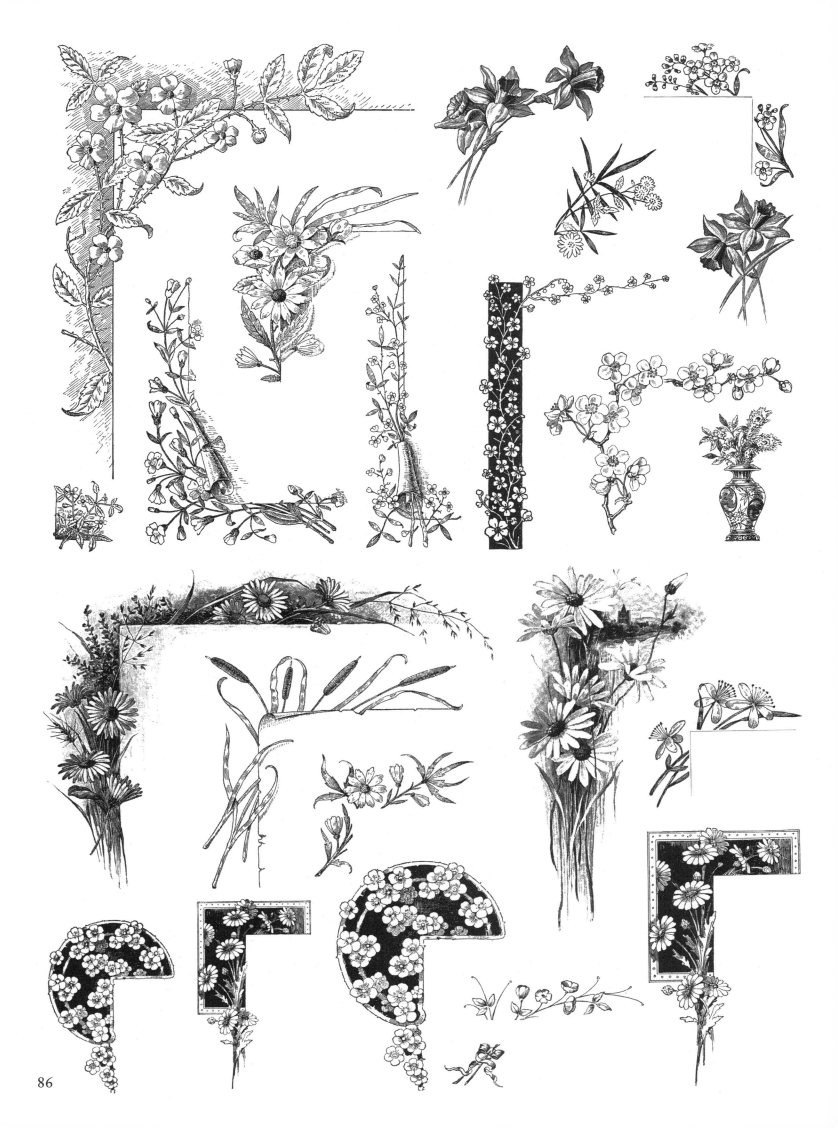

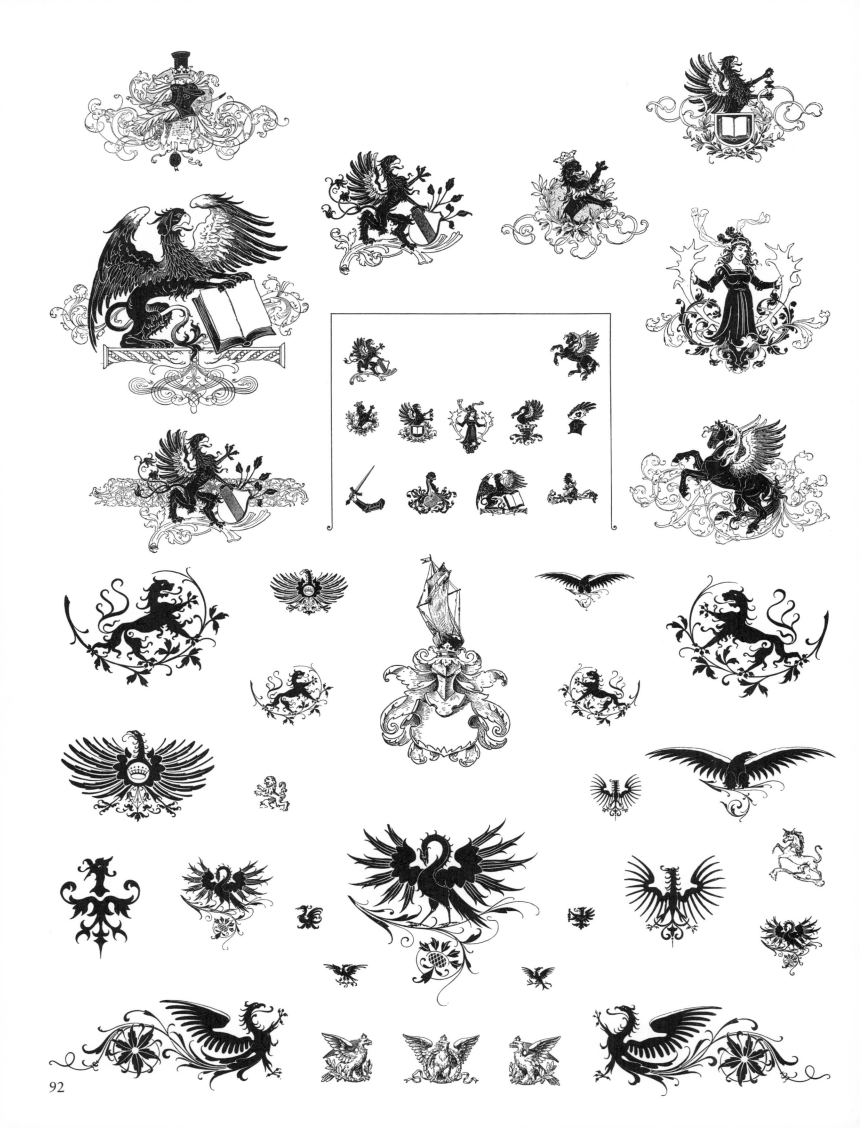

95

96

100

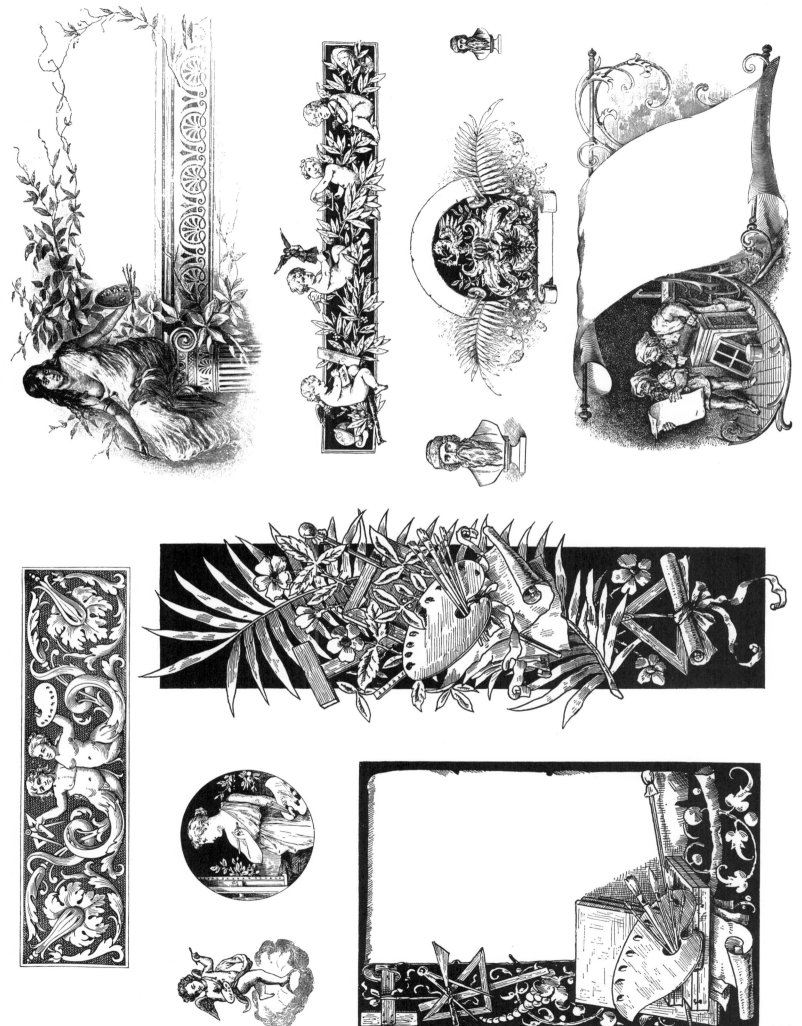

103

105

MENS SANA IN CORPORE SANO

111

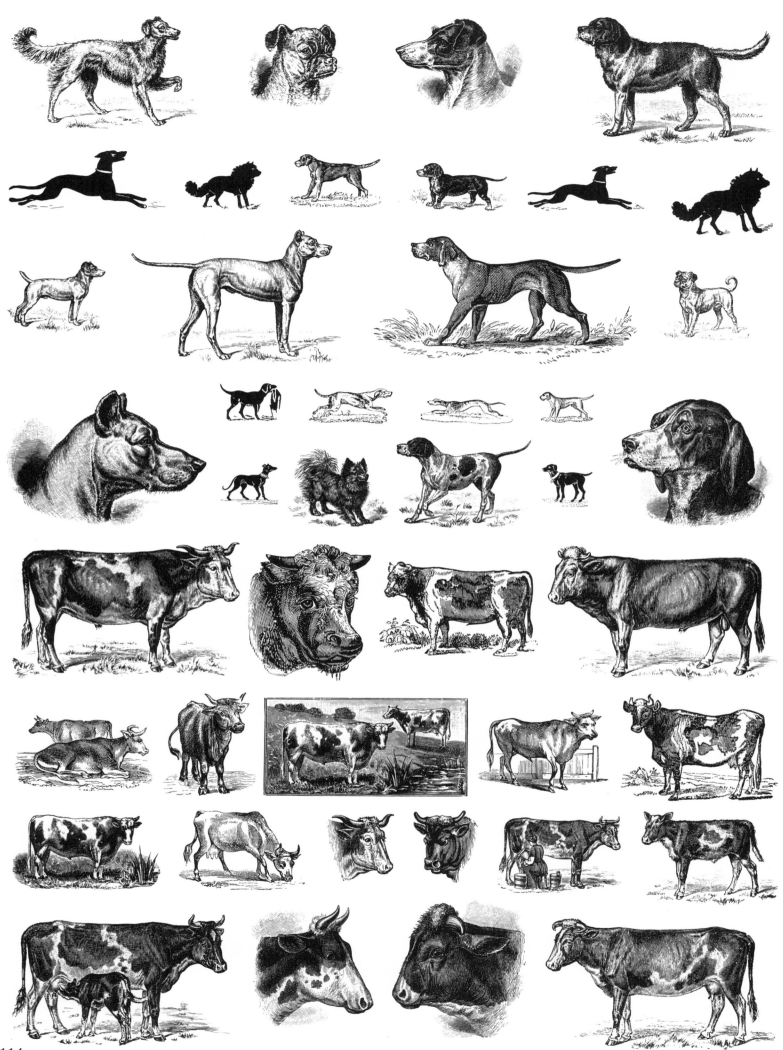

118

119

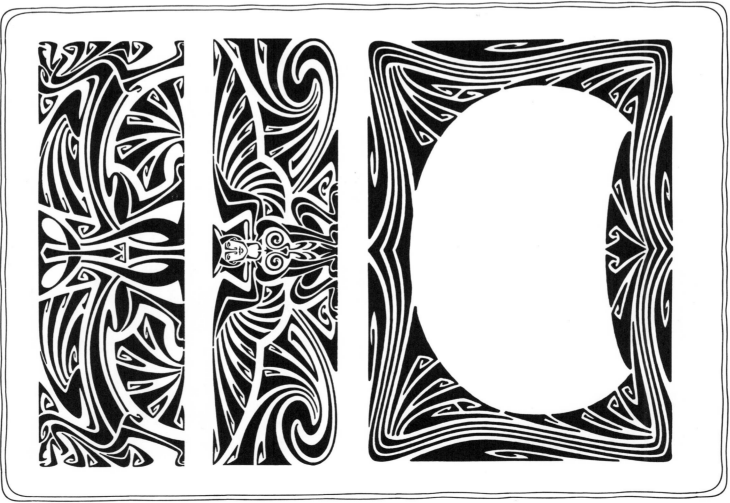